Blueprint for Revival

Blueprint for Revival

How the Health Message Helped
Breathe Life into a Dying Church

F. E. Ramirez, M.D.

Cari Haus

HealthWhys Lifestyle Medicine

Special Thanks
to

Katie Snyder
and
Marko Balaz

for their part in telling this story

and to God

for making it all possible.

CONTENTS

1

Plight of a Dying Church

For many years, the Dundas Seventh-day Adventist Church in Sydney, Australia was the spiritual home for a thriving community of faith. Believers of all age groups gathered there weekly (and frequently in between) to worship, fellowship, and find solace from every-day life.

When long-time member Marko Balaz began attending the Dundas church in 1994, he remembers that there were about 120 active members. The church was an ethnic Croatian church, as members, who were mostly immigrants, spoke their native language in worship services there.

Time had taken a toll, however. As children of the church grew up, the second and third generations either moved away or integrated into English-speaking churches. No one moved in to take their place. Attendance dwindled to the point where, in a beautiful facility with seats enough for 220, there were only 14 church members attending. Most of the members were elderly, and there were other problems as well. The church which had once been so happy became known as a challenging one. Things got so bad there was even talk of closing its doors for good.

Fast Forward Three Years

Fast forward three years (to 2022) and you will find quite a different story. The church is alive and well! Seeker-focused activities take place at their beautiful facility every day of the week. Weekly church attendance, which spans all age groups, is close to a hundred. When the church holds special programs for the community, as many as 80 outside guests happily attend.

What happened that so dramatically transformed this church? The answers are simple. The church followed the instruction God gave, the "blueprint," to turn things around. What is this blueprint? Just a set of transformative (but Biblical) steps that any church body can follow. Those steps are outlined in the following chapters, woven into the story of the Dundas church.

2

Prayer, Willingness & Faith

With membership in such steep decline, leaders of the church had every reason to feel discouraged. Things certainly weren't going well. Yet church leaders didn't despair. Instead of giving up hope, they took matters to God in prayer. Forming a small group to intercede for the congregation, they began praying together at 5:30 on Sunday mornings.

In their Bible study, church leaders had noticed that just before God did something great, prayer was almost always involved. That was just how it rolled. So they prayed—and they prayed for great things.

"We asked earnestly for God's wisdom," Marko says. "Humbly we asked God for guidance—what to do and how to do it. And we believed that He would be with us."

In the 1990's, Marko had experienced a powerful dream about the church. In the dream, he walked up to the front door of the church and found it so crowded that he could hardly get in! Though the church was in steep decline, Marko reminded the other church members about his dream. Feeling encouraged, the other church members adopted Marko's dream so that it became their dream too. Then, they prayed even more.

They Moved Forward in Faith

When membership was at its lowest and talk arose of renting out or even closing the church, the few members on hand chose to take a different route. Believing that God could and would send them more members, they refurbished the church complex inside and out. Being a rather frugal and sacrificial congregation, they were able to pay for the renovations with cash. When they were done, every area of the beautiful church was updated. In addition to the sanctuary, there were now well-planned and thoughtfully furnished offices, children's rooms, a fellowship hall, and even a commercial kitchen.

They Were Open and Willing

For many years, the ministry of the congregation (as ethnic Croatian) had served the community well. As they prayed about the problems facing the church, the leadership began to feel that the church should become more international in nature. They became convicted that, to widen the reach of the church and touch more people, the congregation should become an English-speaking church.

This was no easy decision. The congregation was quite comfortable within their long-time culture. But, after continued prayer and conversation, the choice was made. Then the church members and congregation came together and made the transition happen. None of what followed next could have taken place if the church hadn't been willing to change. But under the guidance of the Holy Spirit, they remained open-minded and enthusiastic—even when that leading wasn't in the direction they personally preferred.

Calling for Help and Planning

A fourth step the leadership took was to ask for help. In their quest to do what was best for the church, they received guidance and assistance from several ministries. Pastor Gary Kent (of the Australian TV program *The Incredible Journey*), who joined the little group for one of their prayer meetings, suggested to Marko that the location of the Dundas church would be ideal as a Bible school. (The Dundas church was in a highly visible place, central to the thriving city of Sydney).

After meeting to consider the matter, church members voted unanimously to move forward with plans for a Bible school. In 2019, the Dundas church arranged for Pastor Louis Torres (who was working with *Adventist World Radio*) and his wife Carol to come over from America and hold a Bible school. While assembling his team, Pastor Torres asked two Bible workers (Katie and Joseph Snyder) to come from New Zealand. Katie had 14 years' experience in the field as a Bible worker, and both of the Snyders were graduates of *Mission College of Evangelism* (which was run by Pastor and Mrs. Torres).

There was just one problem: the Snyders, who were happily living in New Zealand at the time, had no intention of moving to Australia. The couple did, however, have a commitment to go wherever God called them. And when the call came in, go they did!

They Planned Well

With this partnership between Gary Kent, 'The Incredible Journey', Pastor and Mrs. Torres, the Snyders, and one other Bible worker, planning for church growth began in earnest.

As part of their planning, the leadership team divvied up their outreach efforts into a 6-month evangelistic cycle. This 6-month cycle had regular health outreach programs dotted throughout with a harvest evangelistic series planned for the end. The plan was to start offering programs right away, and "dot" them regularly over the six months of the cycle. In addition to health-related programs, there were also regular activities that took place every week such as:

- Wednesdays: Prayer meeting
- Friday evenings: A social time with a bit of singing and some food.
- Sabbath mornings:
    - A Bible School (code name for Sabbath School)
    - The weekly church service (which people were invited to after attending the Bible School)
    - A delicious church potluck every week

"The weekly potluck is not a negotiable thing," says Katie. "It's not good enough to have a great church service and then just say 'Good-bye, have a great week!' You've got to sit down and chat."

"We had a team of very committed and amazing ladies that literally pumped out bucket loads of food," laughs Katie. "To the point where there were 12 basketfuls left over that the Bible workers ate the next week."

"You can't bring people into the church without a hospitality ministry," Katie reiterates. "It's a real pillar in being able to keep people coming. You really need to get to know the people and connect with them."

In addition to the activities and hospitality ministry, the church maintained a calendar of upcoming events in the foyer. In this way, people coming to the church could be made aware of future programs. Announcements about upcoming events were also made weekly from the front of the church.

The entire plan was developed with much prayer.

"Prayer needs to be the basis of the planning," says Katie. "That's not negotiable."

4

Flexing the Right Arm of the Gospel

"There are several tools in the Bible worker's trade," says Katie. "One of the best and most powerful of those, to get things going, is health evangelism." With God's leading and help, the church pulled out that tool, and more.

One of the programs held early on was a health series featuring Dr. Eddie Ramirez (Health Ministries Director for the *Pennsylvania Conference*). People who came to the program, which was called "Dinner with the Doctor," received a delicious meal and the benefit of an interesting health lecture. They were also given a free book, provided they filled out a survey that provided their contact information and stated what kind of programs would interest them in the future. At the beginning of each "Dinner with the Doctor," the pastor would say a few words. When the program was over, church members and others had an opportunity to visit with those who attended.

Regrouping After a Setback

The work of reviving the church was not to be without setbacks. Just as things really got rolling (in March of 2020), the COVID pandemic struck. The Bible school—along with many other potential activities

—were quickly shut down. Australia was particularly strict; virtually everything came to a stop and people were locked inside.

Gary Kent, Pastor Torres and the Bible school attendees faced a difficult choice. Either leave the country, or be stuck there for an extended (and unknown) period of time. After discussing the various options, it seemed best for Pastor Torres and most of the attendees to leave. Only the Snyders remained. For the fledgling project, it looked like "game over."

Instead of becoming discouraged, however, the leadership team regrouped. For a six-week span, they switched their efforts to social media.

"We didn't grow up in the social media era, so the tech side was a real challenge for us," says Katie. Despite the big learning curve (and with God's help), the team was able to implement the tools they needed. One of those tools was online Bible studies. With so many people stuck inside, it just seemed like a good time for that.

From his post overseas, Pastor Torres continued to help. Zoom meetings became the number one form of communication for the little group. Pastor Torres helped with Zoom Sabbath Schools and even filmed an entire Evangelistic series from the US for livestreaming.

The church also offered *Lockdown FastTrack*, a ramped-up Bible study program where Katie studied with people every day instead of once per week. She continued this for six weeks until things opened up again.

"The lockdown was actually a blessing in disguise," Katie explains. "By the time things reopened, we had six people ready for baptism."

After being at home for so long, many from the community were eager to come to programs. Once things finally started opening up again, the Dundas church was one of the first to re-open its doors.

Because only ten people were allowed to gather at a time, the leaders asked church members to stay home and join by live stream. As the government allowed more and more people, they visitors were given priority. Soon they were allowed 20 visitors, then 50. The church members continued to worship by Zoom from home as visitors filled the spaces allowed until the church was able to meet together again.

"We just fed them and continued working with them," says Katie. "It's been a wonderful privilege to see the remarkable things God has done in this church."

5

Praying and Getting Out the Word

As the outreach began picking up steam, the church continued their prayer efforts. The twice daily leadership team prayer meetings (at 7 a.m. and 7 p.m.) continued. Together on Zoom, the church implored God for help. The prayer meeting has continued even after they saw success. It is *not negotiable!*

As Katie says, "nothing happens without praying." So they prayed, continued to pray, and never let up as they worked along through the plan.

Getting Out the Word

Part of the 6-month plan was to have a continuous round of activities being hosted by the church so there was always something to invite people to.

As soon as Australia began to re-open after COVID, the Bible workers went straight to the doors. Another Bible worker joined the team at this point and added her giftings to the mix. They each spent about 20 hours per week inviting people to the programs, but they didn't do it alone. Whenever possible they added church members to their team and split into twos, thereby doubling their efforts. Although some flyers and letters were mailed out, most of the invitation work was done in person. Hundreds of phone calls, text messages and visits made each initiative a thorough saturation of the community.

"People are far more likely to come when you look them in the eye to invite them," says Katie. "Most of what comes in the mail is just junk anyway, and quickly thrown out."

"You have to market what you've got," says Katie. "You might have something fabulous planned, but if you don't tell the community, you'll go nowhere. It will be a waste of time."

One of the men who visited the Dundas church was so impressed with what was going on he volunteered his expertise in the area of technical support. He assisted to manage and design social media platforms Facebook and YouTube. He also helped with flyer design and even setup QR codes (which when scanned direct a person to the website).

"My husband and I aren't very tech savvy," says Katie. "But its very important to maximize the power of more up-to-date methods and get the word out. We did what we could, and God blessed."

One of the blessings the church received was the opportunity to be a COVID test site during the pandemic. As people arrived for testing, they got to drive by signs the church put up to advertise upcoming programs. In addition to the added visibility, the church was blessed by the extra funds given them by the government for providing this service. Those funds were used to further the mission of the church in the community

6

Calling for--and Receiving--More Help

"More workers" was one of the things the church prayed urgently for right from the start. In doing so, they were simply following the advice of Jesus (Matthew 9:37-38), where He counseled His followers that "The harvest truly is great, but the labourers are few: pray ye therefore the Lord of the harvest, that he would send forth labourers into his harvest." The Dundas church took this counsel to heart.

"Lord, please send us more help," was frequent prayer ascending to heaven.

God heard and answered those prayers—sometimes from unexpected places. Once, while Marko and his wife were attending a birthday party, a former Adventist came and told them, "If I come back to church, I'd like to be very involved." The very next Sabbath she came to church.

"I told you, if I come back, I want to be involved," the lady reminded them. Marko's wife responded with an embrace and a hug.

"Welcome back! We are very happy to have you!" And so a new member, and very active helper, was added to the team.

Another lady was added to the team, followed a year later by two youth workers, one of which was from Papua, New Guinea. A young lady who speaks Chinese Mandarin was also added. Soon there were five Bible workers altogether, working on sacrificial stipends.

Each member of this "little army of Bible workers" was blessed with different talents. The Chinese Bible worker helped a retired couple open the church for ping pong two days per week. At the same time, English and greeting card classes took place. One of the Bible workers, who was 60 years old but very fitness oriented, started a weekly fitness boot-camp that ran every Sunday morning. Another Bible worker started the *Journey to Wholeness* program to help people with addictions.

Other programs the church team offered included:

- A weekly cooking school called *Meals that Heal*
- The *Depression Recovery Program* and a follow-up called *Learning to Tell Yourself the Truth*
- Two care groups for people to come, eat, talk and feel cared for
- A class called *How to Forgive*, and
- Personal coaching.

As the evangelism cycle progressed, door-to-door work continued to be a big part of the plan.

"There's always someone we are trying to meet," says Katie, adding that they were totally "seeker focused" in the work. Some of the programs the team decided to do were based on community need. If 2-3 people said they wanted a program, the church did it. This church is so busy they literally have programs every single day of the week!

7

Building on Success

As the 6-month evangelism cycle progressed, the church continued hosting (and inviting the community to) their programs.

At the end of one evangelistic cycle, Dr. Eddie Ramirez (who had presented a *Dinner with the Doctor* series in 2019 just before the pandemic struck) returned for another series.

As they had been doing all along, the Bible worker Team went door-to-door to let people know of the upcoming program.

"We've got a doctor coming from Pennsylvania who's worked in life-style centers for more than 28 years," Katie told the people. "Come and hear what he has to say!"

And come they did! In addition to the ever-growing group of church members, a total of 145 (mostly visitors) attended the program. The church was so packed! While some church members were shocked at the large attendance, those from the early days were reminded of Marko's dream.

"Marko, your dream has come true!" they told him. And it was so. Marko was elated.

"I had to wait 25 years," he said. "But finally, it happened!"

The goal of the "Dinner with the Doctor" program was to invite every single person who came to attend a weeklong health series that followed the event. At the end people were invited to the upcoming harvest evangelistic meetings. Once again, the goal the group set was met.

Reaping the Harvest

When the evangelistic series began, 60-80 people attended every night. The members were shocked to see so many, but Katie was not.

"Winning souls is all very strategic," says Katie. "Just like planting a garden. In the beginning, the plant just peeks its head above the soil. Pretty soon, it gets going and puts up little shoots. Then it really starts growing. In the beginning, we start with the health programs. We find interests and get to know more and more people. By the time we are ready for harvest, things really start to grow."

"Australia is a very secular country," adds Marko. "But when you follow God's blueprint, the Lord is willing and able to do a fantastic work."

Which is how, in place of a once-dying church, there is now a thriving, international church.

"Today only 5% of church members are from a Croatian background," estimates Marko. "Australia is a very diverse country, and our church reflects that fact. We have members with roots in Iran, India, Samoa, Fiji, Latin America, Africa, and European countries. Basically, from all over the world."

"For everything we give glory to God," says Marko. "He is the one who is worthy."

And that is how an ethnic, mostly elderly congregation grew from a low of 14 attending, to between 80-120 weekly attendance in just three years, pandemic notwithstanding. In addition, more people are ready to make decisions in the next evangelistic meetings.

"God is leading!" says Katie, adding that "with God's help, this success can be repeated by other churches. This isn't just a 'good method.' This *is* the blueprint that should be followed. And when we follow the Blueprint under the guiding and directing of the Holy Spirit the results are astonishing! We are all just ordinary people who made ourselves available for God to do extraordinary things."

Marko agrees.

"I would like to encourage everyone who hears our story to know that their church can do this too," he says. "Just submit yourselves to the mighty hand of God. Ask Him for guidance. Then be ready to lead wherever He guides you. The Lord is willing and able to do a fantastic work!"

"This model can be applied in other places," Katie reiterates. "And it is definitely worth repeating. In fact, it's the blueprint. The health ministry is the right arm of the gospel. People are interested in health. But we just need to go out there and utilize that right arm. So you are invited to pray about this, and start applying these principles. Then you will see that God will bless tremendously. We need to be busy working, we must be about our Father's business, because of the time we are at in this world's history. Time is short! And it's a blessing to be in this work!"

Amen and Amen.

Following is a summary of the "blueprint" which, if followed carefully and prayerfully, can bring the same results and blessings as those experienced by the Dundas Church:

1. Pray for revival. Pray a lot, and recruit other church members to pray with you at a regular time or times each week.
2. Have faith and never give up. God is in the business of turning the waste places of the earth--and human hearts--into beautiful gardens that glorify Him.
3. Step forward in faith and, as far as able, prepare your church facility for the growth that will come.
4. Ask God--and sister ministries--for help. Pray for God to send the workers.
5. Develop a 6-month evangelism plan that:
   a. Begins with health evangelism or other helping ministries that will enable your team to better connect with the community.
   b. Best utilizes the specific talents of church members (and others God sends).
   c. Includes a hospitality ministry (good, healthy meals served in a friendly atmosphere).
   d. Keeps the church doors open for activities as many days of the week as possible.
6. Get the word out about the programs your church is hosting.
   a. Utilize Facebook and other social media platforms to the best of your ability.

    b. Personal invitations are always best!

7. Pray your way through any adversity.

    a. Challenges will surely arise, since the devil won't like what you're doing.

    b. Keep the prayer meetings going and, as needed, ramp them up when obstacles arise.

8. Learn from your experiences and start a new 6-month evangelism plan as the first one ends.

    a. Interactions with the community should tell you what types of programs they prefer. Start new programs to meet the needs of your specific community as they become clear.

    b. Invite everyone who comes to the programs to attend your church.

    c. Cultivate a warm and welcoming atmosphere in church each Sabbath.

That's it! May God bless your efforts and those of your church with many new members as you implement this "Blueprint for Revival."

The Importance of Caring for Our Bodies

"Know ye not that your body is the temple of the Holy Ghost which is in you, which ye have of God, and ye are not your own? For ye are bought with a price; therefore glorify God in your body, and in your spirit, which are God's." (1 Corinthians 6:19-20)

"Whether therefore ye eat, or drink, or whatsoever ye do, do all to the glory of God." (1 Corinthians 10:31)

"I will praise thee; for I am fearfully and wonderfully made: marvellous are thy works; and that my soul knoweth right well." (Psalm 139:14)

"And take heed to yourselves, lest at any time your hearts be overcharged with surfeiting, and drunkenness, and cares of this life, and so that day come upon you unawares." (Luke 21:34)

"And put a knife to thy throat, if thou be a man given to appetite. Be not desirous of his dainties: for they are deceitful meat." (Proverbs 23:2-3)

"I beseech you therefore, brethren, by the mercies of God, that ye present your bodies a living sacrifice, holy, acceptable unto God, which is your reasonable service." (Romans 12:1)

The Godly will be Temperate

"But the fruit of the Spirit is love, joy, peace, longsuffering, gentleness, goodness, faith, meekness, temperance: against such there is no law." - Galatians 5:22-23

Blessed art thou, O land, when thy king is the son of nobles, and thy princes eat in due season, for strength, and not for drunkenness!" (Ecclesiastes 10:17)

"Know ye not that they which run in a race run all, but one receiveth the prize? So run, that ye may obtain. And every man that striveth for the mastery is temperate in all things. Now they do it to obtain a corruptible crown; but we an incorruptible. I therefore so run, not as uncertainly; so fight I, not as one that beateth the air: But I keep under my body, and bring it into subjection: lest that by any means, when I have preached to others, I myself should be a castaway." (1 Corinthians 9:24-27)

"Know ye not that the unrighteous shall not inherit the kingdom of God? Be not deceived: neither fornicators, nor idolaters, nor adulterers, nor effeminate, nor abusers of themselves with mankind, Nor thieves, nor covetous, nor drunkards, nor revilers, nor extortioners, shall inherit the kingdom of God." (1 Corinthians 6:9-10)

Healing of Body and Soul are Closely Related

"Is any sick among you? let him call for the elders of the church; and let them pray over him, anointing him with oil in the name of the Lord: And the prayer of faith shall save the sick, and the Lord shall raise him up; and if he have committed sins, they shall be forgiven him. Confess your faults one to another, and pray one for another, that ye may be healed. The effectual fervent prayer of a righteous man availeth much." (James 5:14-16)

"When Jesus saw their faith, he said unto the sick of the palsy, Son, thy sins be forgiven thee. But there was certain of the scribes sitting there, and reasoning in their hearts, Why doth this man thus speak blasphemies? who can forgive sins but God only? And immediately when Jesus perceived in his spirit that they so reasoned within themselves, he said unto them, Why reason ye these things in your hearts? Whether is it easier to say to the sick of the palsy, Thy sins be forgiven thee; or to say, Arise, and take up thy bed, and walk? But that ye may know that the Son of man hath power on earth to forgive sins, (he saith to the sick of the palsy,) I say unto thee, Arise, and take up thy bed, and go thy way into thine house." (Mark 2:5-11)

"Having therefore these promises, dearly beloved, let us cleanse ourselves from all filthiness of the flesh and spirit, perfecting holiness in the fear of God." (2 Corinthians 7:1)

"Be not wise in thine own eyes: fear the LORD, and depart from evil. It shall be health to thy navel, and marrow to thy bones." (Proverbs 3:7-8)

God, the Great Healer, Wants Us to be Healthy

"Beloved, I wish above all things that thou mayest prosper and be in health, even as thy soul prospereth." (3 John 2)

"He giveth power to the faint; and to them that have no might he increaseth strength. Even the youths shall faint and be weary, and the young men shall utterly fall: But they that wait upon the LORD shall renew their strength; they shall mount up with wings as eagles; they shall run, and not be weary; and they shall walk, and not faint." (Isaiah 40:29-31)

"Bless the Lord, O my soul, and forget not all his benefits: Who forgiveth all thine iniquities; who healeth all thy diseases..." (Psalm 103:2-3)

Jesus was a Great Healer

"And Jesus went about all Galilee, teaching in their synagogues, and preaching the gospel of the kingdom, and healing all manner of sickness and all manner of disease among the people." (Matthew 4:23)

"For even hereunto were ye called: because Christ also suffered for us, leaving us an example, that ye should follow his steps:" (1 Peter 2:21)

"When the even was come, they brought unto him many that were possessed with devils: and he cast out the spirits with his word, and healed all that were sick: That it might be fulfilled which was spoken by Esaias the prophet, saying, Himself took our infirmities, and bare our sicknesses." (Matthew 8:16-17)

The Disciples Engaged in Healing

"And they cast out many devils, and anointed with oil many that were sick, and healed them." (Mark 6:13)

"And when he had called unto him his twelve disciples, he gave them power against unclean spirits, to cast them out, and to heal all manner of sickness and all manner of disease." (Matthew 10:1)

"And he ordained twelve, that they should be with him, and that he might send them forth to preach, And to have power to heal sicknesses, and to cast out devils:" (Mark 3:14-15)

"Then he called his twelve disciples together, and gave them power and authority over all devils, and to cure diseases. And he sent them to preach the kingdom of God, and to heal the sick." (Luke 9:1-2)

"After these things the Lord appointed other seventy also, and sent them two and two before his face into every city and place, whither he himself would come...And heal the sick that are therein, and say unto them, The kingdom of God is come nigh unto you." (Luke 10:1-9)

Natural Remedies Were Part of Bible Healings

"He answered and said, A man that is called Jesus made clay, and anointed mine eyes, and said unto me, Go to the pool of Siloam, and wash: and I went and washed, and I received sight." (John 9:11)

"And Isaiah said, Take a lump of figs. And they took and laid it on the boil, and he recovered." (2 Kings 20:7)

"And went to him, and bound up his wounds, pouring in oil and wine, and set him on his own beast, and brought him to an inn, and took care of him." (Luke 10:34)

"And by the river upon the bank thereof, on this side and on that side, shall grow all trees for meat, whose leaf shall not fade, neither shall the fruit thereof be consumed: it shall bring forth new fruit according to his months, because their waters they issued out of the sanctuary: and the fruit thereof shall be for meat, and the leaf thereof for medicine." (Ezekiel 47:12)

Promises of Health and Healing for the Faithful

"And ye shall serve the Lord your God, and he shall bless thy bread, and thy water; and I will take sickness away from the midst of thee." - Exodus 23:25

"For I will restore health unto thee, and I will heal thee of thy wounds, saith the Lord." (Jeremiah 30:17)

"The Lord will keep you free from every disease. He will not inflict on you the horrible diseases you knew in Egypt." (Exodus 15:26)

"Blessed be the Lord, who daily loadeth us with benefits, even the God of our salvation." (Psalm 68:19)

Believers are Called to Share the Gospel (including the Health Message)

"And Jesus came and spake unto them, saying, All power is given unto me in heaven and in earth. Go ye therefore, and teach all nations, baptizing them in the name of the Father, and of the Son, and of the Holy Ghost: Teaching them to observe all things whatsoever I have commanded you: and, lo, I am with you always, even unto the end of the world. Amen." (Matthew 28:18-20)

"And said unto them, Thus it is written, and thus it behoved Christ to suffer, and to rise from the dead the third day: And that repentance and remission of sins should be preached in his name among all nations, beginning at Jerusalem. And ye are witnesses of these things. And, behold, I send the promise of my Father upon you: but tarry ye in the city of Jerusalem, until ye be endued with power from on high." (Luke 24:46-49)

"Harness the horses; and get up, ye horsemen, and stand forth with your helmets; furbish the spears, and put on the brigandines." (Jeremiah 46:4)

"Bear ye one another's burdens, and so fulfil the law of Christ." (Galatians 6:2)

"We then that are strong ought to bear the infirmities of the weak, and not to please ourselves." (Romans 15:1)

"Withhold not good from them to whom it is due, when it is in the power of thine hand to do it." (Proverbs 3:27)

A Continuance of Christ's Work

"Christ is no longer in this world in person, to go through our cities and town and villages, healing the sick; but He has commissioned us to carry forward the medical missionary work that He began." (*Testimonies for the Church* vol. 9 p. 168)

"Christ's servants are to follow His example. As He went from place to place, He comforted the suffering and healed the sick. Then He placed before them the great truths in regard to His kingdom. This is the work of His followers." (*Christ's Object Lessons* pp. 233-234)

"Christ's method alone will give true success in reaching the people. The Savior, mingled with men as one who desired their good. He showed His sympathy for them, ministered to their needs, and won their confidence. Then He bade them, 'Follow me.'" (*Ministry of Healing* p. 734)

The Health – Spirituality Connection

"Health is a blessing of which few appreciate the value; yet upon it the efficiency of our mental and physical powers largely depends. Our impulses and passions have their seat in the body, and it must be kept in the best condition physically and under the most spiritual influences in order that our talents may be put to the highest use. Anything that lessens physical strength enfeebles the mind and makes it less capable of discriminating between right and wrong. We become less capable of choosing the good and have less strength of will to do that which we know to be right." (*Christ's Object Lessons* p. 346)

"Transgression of physical law is transgression of the moral law; for God is as truly the author of physical laws as He is the author of the moral law. His law is written with His own finger upon every nerve, every muscle, every faculty, which has been entrusted to man. And every misuse of any part of our organism is a violation of that law." (*Christ's Object Lessons* pp. 347-348)

The Work of Every Member

"All need to become acquainted with that most wonderful of all organisms, the human body...They should study the influence of the mind upon the body and of the body upon the mind, and the laws by which they are governed." (*Ministry of Healing* p. 128)

"All gospel workers should know how to give the simple treatments that do so much to relieve pain and remove disease." (*Ministry of Healing* p. 146)

"We have come to a time when every member of the church should take hold of medical missionary work. The world is a lazar house filled with victims of both physical and spiritual disease. Everywhere people are perishing for lack of a knowledge of the truths that have been committed to us. The members of the church are in need of an awakening, that they may realize their responsibility to impart these truths." (*Testimonies for the Church* vol. 7 p. 62)

Those who take up this line of work [circulating publications] are to go prepared to do medical missionary work. The sick and suffering are to be helped. Many for whom this work of mercy is done will hear and accept the words of life. (*Testimonies for the Church* vol. 9 p. 34)

"Let our people show that they have a living interest in medical missionary work. Let them prepare themselves for usefulness by studying the books that have been written for our instruction in these lines. These books deserve much more attention and appreciation than they have received." (*Testimonies for the Church* vo. 7 p. 63)

The Work of Every Church

"There is a message regarding health reform to be borne in every church." (*Testimonies for the Church* vol. 6 p. 370)

"The medical missionary work should be a part of the work of every church in our land." (*Testimonies for the Church* vol 6 p. 289)

Workers Urged to Go Forward

"Let them take the living principle of health reform into the communities that to a large degree are ignorant of these principles." (*Testimonies for the Church* vol. 9 p. 118)

"I am instructed to say to health reform educators, Go forward. The world needs every jot of the influence you can exert to press back the tide of moral woe. Let those who teach the third angel's message stand true to their colors." (*Testimonies for the Church* vol. 9 p. 113)

A Source of Great Spiritual Strength

"Nothing will give greater spiritual strength and a greater increase of earnestness and depth of feeling, than visiting and ministering to the sick and the desponding, helping them to see the light and to fasten their faith upon Jesus." (*Testimonies for the Church* vol. 4 pp. 75-76)

The Blueprint for Revival

"Get the young men and women in the churches to work. Combine medical missionary work with the proclamation of the third angel's message. Make regular, organized efforts to lift the church members out of the dead level in which they have been for years. Send out into the churches workers who will live the principles of health reform. Let those be sent who can see the necessity of self-denial in appetite, or they will be a snare to the church. See if the breath of life will not then come into our churches." (*Testimonies for the Church* vol. 6 p. 267)

A Great Soother of Nerves

"The influence of the Spirit of God is the very best medicine for disease. Heaven is all health; the more deeply heavenly influences are realized, the more sure will be the recovery of the believing invalid." (*Counsels to Parents, Teachers and Students* p. 13)

"Sickness of the mind prevails everywhere. Nine tenths of the diseases from which men suffer have their foundation here. Perhaps some living home trouble is, like a canker, eating to the very soul and weakening the life forces. Remorse for sin sometimes undermines the constitution and unbalances the mind. There are erroneous doctrines also, as that of an eternally burning hell and the endless torment of the wicked, that, by giving exaggerated and distorted views of the character of God, have produced the same result upon sensitive minds. Infidels have made the most of these unfortunate cases, attributing insanity to religion; but this is a gross libel and one which they will not be pleased to meet by and by. The religion of Christ, so far from being the cause of insanity, is one of its most effectual remedies; for it is a potent soother of the nerves." (*Testimonies for the Church* vol. 5 p. 443)

"Through His servants, God designs that the sick, the unfortunate, and those possessed of evil spirits, shall hear His voice. Through His human agencies He desires to be a comforter such as the world knows not." (*Ministry of Healing* p. 106)

Intertwined with the Gospel Work

"The light God has given on health reform is for our salvation and the salvation of the world." (*Counsels on Health* p. 446)

"He (God) did not wish the medical missionary work to be separated from the gospel work, or the gospel work separated from the medical missionary work. These are to blend. The medical missionary work is to be regarded as the pioneer work. It is to be the means of breaking down prejudice. As the right arm, it is to open doors for the gospel message." (*Manuscript Release 6* p. 310)

"The medical missionary work is to be to the work of the church as the right arm to the body. The third angel goes forth proclaiming the commandments of God and the faith of Jesus. The medical missionary work is the gospel in practice. All lines of work are to be harmoniously blended in giving the invitation: 'Come; for all things are now ready.'" (Testimonies for the Church vol. 8 p. 77)

"It (the health work) should stand forth with scientific ability, with moral and spiritual power, and as a faithful sentinel of reform in all its bearings; and all who act a part in it should be reformers." (*Counsels on Health* p. 401)

The Right Hand, Door Opener, and Entering Wedge

"Medical missionary work is the right hand of the gospel. It is necessary to the advancement of the cause of God. As through it men and women are led to see the importance of right habits of living, the saving power of the truth will be made known. Every city is to be entered by workers trained to do medical missionary work. As the right hand of the third angel's message, God's methods of treating disease will open doors for the entrance of present truth." (*Testimonies for the Church* vol. 7 p. 59)

"Christ's example must be followed by those who claim to be His children. Relieve the physical necessities of your fellow men, and their gratitude will break down the barriers, and enable you to reach their hearts. Consider this matter earnestly." (*Testimonies for the Church* vol. 9 p. 127)

"The work of health reform is the Lord's means for lessening suffering in our world and for purifying His church. Teach the people that they can act as God's helping hand, by co-operating with the Master Worker in restoring physical and spiritual health. This work bears the signature of Heaven, and will open doors for the entrance of other precious truths. There is room for all to labor who will take hold of this work intelligently.' (*Testimonies for the Church* vol. 9 pp. 112-113)

"First meet the temporal necessities of the needy, and relieve their physical wants and sufferings, and you will then find an open avenue to the heart, where you may plant the good seeds of virtue and religion." (*Testimonies for the Church* vol. 4 p. 227)

"First meet the temporal necessities of the needy and relieve their physical wants and sufferings, and you will then find an open avenue to the heart, where you may plant the good seeds of virtue and religion." (*Testimonies for the Church* vol. 7 p. 227)

"Many not of our faith are longing for the very help that Christians are in duty bound to give. If God's people would show a genuine interest in their neighbors, many would be reached by the special truths for this time. Nothing will or ever can give character to the work like helping the people just where they are. Thousands might today be rejoicing in the message, if those who claim to love God and keep His commandments would work as Christ worked. When the medical missionary work thus wins men and women to a saving knowledge of Christ and His truth, money and earnest labor may safely be invested in it; for it is a work that will endure." (*Testimonies for the Church* vol. 6 p. 280)

"Medical missionary work is in no case to be divorced from the gospel ministry. The Lord has specified that the two shall be as closely connected as the arm is with the body. Without this union neither part of the work is complete. The medical missionary work is the gospel in illustration." (*Counsels on Health* p. 524)

The Urgency of the Work

"I have been instructed that the medical missionary work will discover, in the very depths of degradation, men who, though they have given themselves up to intemperate, dissolute habits, will respond to the right kind of labor. But they need to be recognized and encouraged. Firm, patient, earnest effort will be required in order to lift them up. They cannot restore themselves. They may hear Christ's call, but their ears are too dull to take in its meaning; their eyes are too blind to see anything good in store for them. They are dead in trespasses and sins. Yet even these are not to be excluded from the gospel feast. They are to receive the invitation, "Come." Though they may feel unworthy, the Lord says, "Compel them to come in." Listen to no excuse. By love and kindness lay right hold of them." (*Testimonies for the Church* vol. 6 pp. 279-80)

"Let the Lord's work go forward. Let the medical missionary and the educational work go forward. I am sure that this is our great lack, —earnest, devoted, intelligent, capable workers." (*Testimonies for the Church* vol. 9 pp. 168-169)

Can Do Much More Good then the Ministry Alone

"I have been surprised at being asked by physicians if I did not think it would be more pleasing to God for them to give up their medical practice and enter the ministry. I am prepared to answer such an inquirer: If you are a Christian and a competent physician, you are qualified to do tenfold more good as a missionary for God than if you were to go forth merely as a preacher of the word." (*Counsels on Health* p. 503)

"Some utterly fail to realize the importance of missionaries being also medical missionaries. A gospel minister will be twice as successful in his work if he understands how to treat disease....A minister of the gospel, who is also a medical missionary, who can cure physical ailments, is a much more efficient worker than one who cannot do this. His work as a minister of the gospel is much more complete." (*Medical Ministry* p. 245)

A River of Life for God's Goodness

"Medical missionary work and the gospel ministry are the channels through which God seeks to pour a constant supply of His goodness. They are to be as the river of life for the irrigation of His church." (*Bible Echo*, Aug. 12, 1901)

The Pioneer Work of the Gospel

"Medical missionary work is the pioneer work of the gospel. In the ministry of the word and in the medical missionary work the gospel is to be preached and practiced." (*Ministry of Healing* p. 144)

The Way to Reach Large Cities

"Henceforth medical missionary work is to be carried forward with an earnestness with which it has never yet been carried. This work is the door through which the truth is to find entrance to the large cities." (*Testimonies for the Church* vol. 9 p. 167)

The Only Line of Work Allowed at the Very End

"I wish to tell you that soon there will be no work done in ministerial lines but medical missionary work." (*Counsels on Health* p. 533)

"As religious aggression subverts the liberties of our nation, those who would stand for freedom of conscience will be placed in unfavorable positions. For their own sake, they should, while they have opportunity, become intelligent in regard to disease, its causes, prevention, and cure. And those who do this will find a field of labor anywhere. There will be suffering ones, plenty of them, who will need help, not only among those of our own faith, but largely among those who know not the truth." (*Counsels on Health* p. 506)

Promises of Blessing, Success & Supernatural Results

"If we do our part in faith, God will open ways before us now undreamed of." (*Selected Messages* vol. 2 p. 206)

"Natural means, used in accordance with God's will, bring about supernatural results. We ask for a miracle, and the Lord directs the mind to some simple remedy. We ask to be kept from the pestilence that walketh in darkness, that is stalking with such power through the world; we are then to cooperate with God." (*Selected Messages* vol. 2 p. 346)

"Much that is for the benefit of all to understand has been written for the special purpose of instruction in the principles of health. Those who study and practice these principles will be greatly blessed, both physically and spiritually." (*Testimonies for the Church* vo. 7 p. 63)

"Had you carried the work forward in the lines in which God intended you to, had you done medical missionary work, trying to heal soul and body, you would have seen hundreds and thousands coming into the truth." (*1888 Study Materials* p. 1750)

What?

"Dinner with the Doctor" evenings are instructional programs developed to educate people on how to implement a whole food, plant based approach for treating, preventing and reversing disease. They are also a fun and informative way to:

- Share a delicious, plant-based meal with local community members
- Introduce friends and acquaintances to the tastiness of a delicious, whole food, plant-based meal
- Get to know friends and neighbors better

Where?

While often held in schools or church fellowship halls, "Dinner with the Doctor" programs can take place anywhere with adequate seating, parking, and food preparation facility to handle a group of people.

When?

"Dinner with the Doctor" usually takes place during the evening meal. In some places "Breakfast with the Doctor" has been a successful program, especially on the weekends.

Who?

The team for a "Dinner with the Doctor" program normally includes:

- A physician / presenter who is familiar with healthy living and lifestyle medicine*
- A sponsoring organization (such as a church or school) to provide the place, funding, and public relations for the event
- A chef or team of cooks to prepare and serve a delicious, plant-based meal
- The minister (or ministry team) of the local church, together with supporting church members, to host and connect with attendees
- Follow-up team. A survey should be taken at the beginning or end of the event asking attendees what interests they have. Would they like to learn in the near future about a specific topic such as diabetes, hypertension, depression, obesity, etc.? Would they like to have a better family? Better finances? Start Bible studies? That way you can plan future programs that meet those community needs. By obtaining participants' contact information, you will also be able to invite them to the events they are interested in, when they are offered.

How?

Although there are several different ways these programs can be presented, they often include:

- A free, delicious, healthy plant-based meal
- A free book given at the end to those who complete a survey which states what type of other programs might interest them

- Sometimes the doctor presents during the meal, sometimes during dessert or after the meal
- The doctor's lecture is usually about 45 minutes long, with an opportunity for questions at the end
- Depending on the choices of the organizers, sometimes there is:
  - A charge for the meal
  - Required pre-registration
  - The opportunity to make a donation to help cover costs

Throughout the world, there are many dedicated physicians, health professionals and health educators with an excellent knowledge of lifestyle medicine who could speak at these types of events. Dr. Eddie Ramirez, the Executive Director for *Adventist WholeHealth Network* is doing multiple programs in his state.

To contact Dr. Ramirez send an email to eddierd@gmail.com. Examples of topics Dr. Ramirez has presented, with a good response, include:

- Evidence-based Steps for Building a Stronger Immune System

- The Next Pandemic

- Inflammation and How it Affects Your Health

- Epigenetics and Lifestyle

- My Research about Depression and Anxiety

- Heart Disease: The #1 Killer

- Neuroplasticity and How to Harness It

- The Impact of Social Connections and Mental and Physical Health

- Chronobiology and Your Health

Watch the YouTube video that inspired this book!

www.ingramcontent.com/pod-product-compliance
Lightning Source LLC
Chambersburg PA
CBHW070947120626
46546CB00004B/1606